Bunky Tries to do the Dishes

Life with Bunky: 8

Written and photographed by:

Diane Baxter Trapeni

Keep an eye out for these other exciting titles:

Nellie the Nibbler

Alice the Guinea Pig

Penny the Python

Jeremiah, a Song Bird

Vincent

Hubert

Phil Harmonic

Jeff Sticks up for his Buddies

Cord, Glue and 8 Screws

A Three Piggie Circus

DEDICATION

To my sister Pamela, who loves to clean that kitchen!! I'll love you forever!

DMBT

Bunky switched chores with Jerry.

Now Bunky has to do the dishes (NOT the toilet)!

He wanted to earn his dime for an ice cream cone this week!

(Maybe he'd try Peach ice cream this time.)

Jerry has the toilet cleaning
now!
Bunky is so happy, he did a
dance.

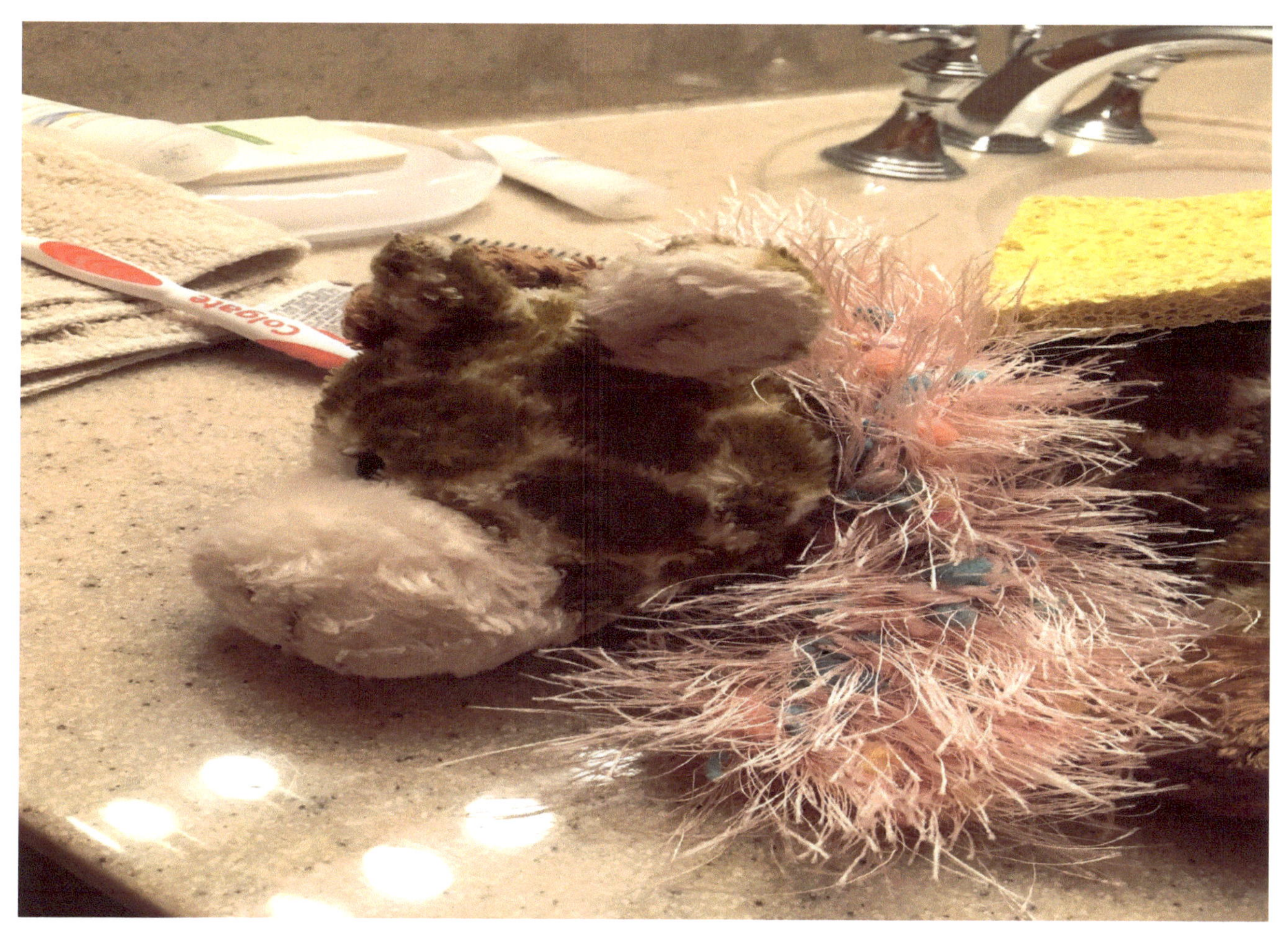

Jerry is not sure he made a good trade yet. Sometimes he makes "bad" choices.

Bunky looked at the sink FULL of greasy, caked-on, yucky dishes.

It made him feel a little queasy.

He had no idea how to do the dishes. He didn't know where to begin. He decided to empty the sink and start all over.

Aurora saw his puzzled look and said she would help him.
She got a tall chair.

Together they rinsed the dishes…one by one. They work together well!

Together they filled the
dishwasher.

It reminded Aurora of a
bucket brigade.

First, the big plates and cookware went in.

Then, the small dishes
and bowls went in.

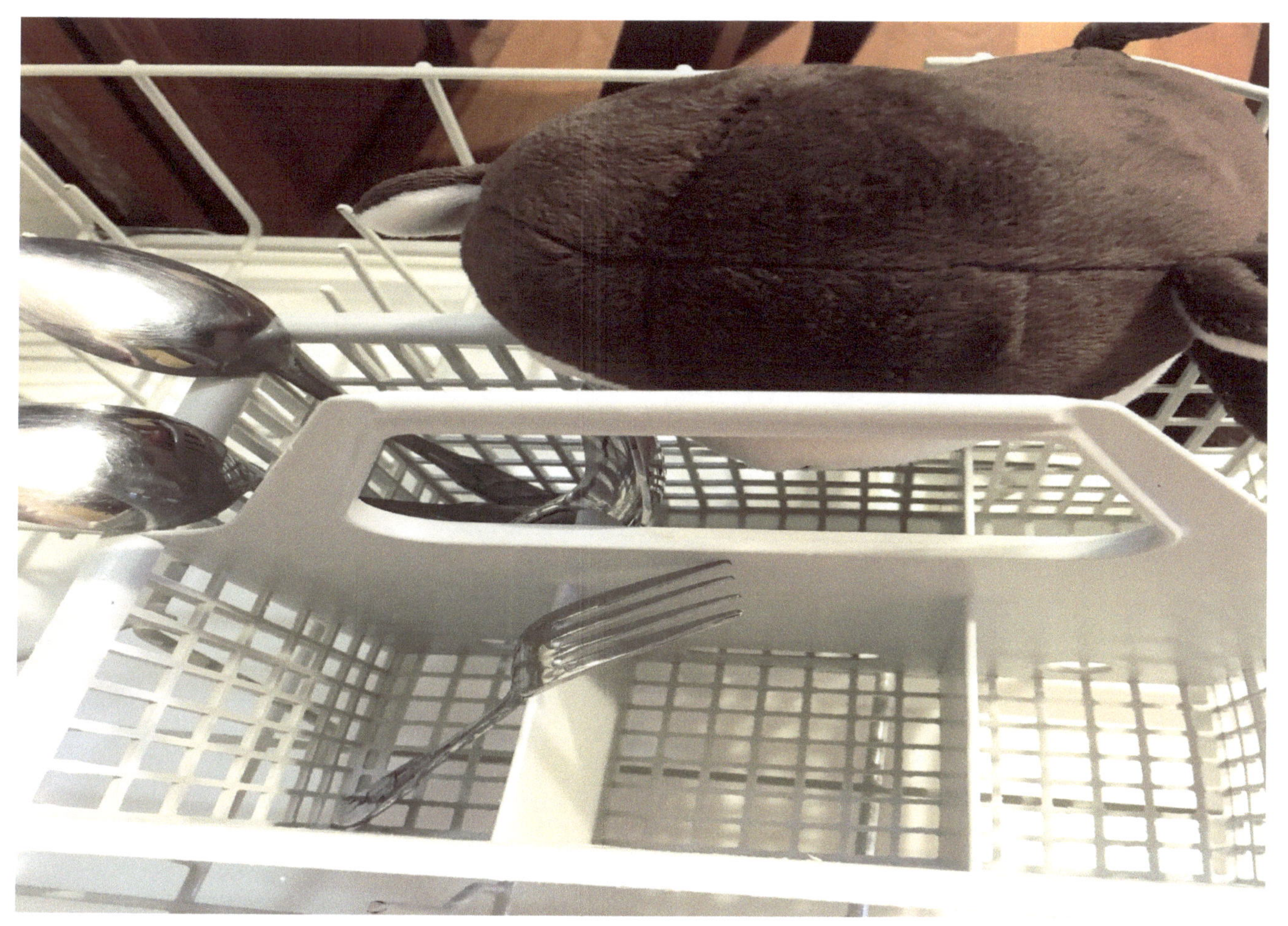

And lastly, they put the forks, spoons and knives in, CAREFULLY! All the knives were put in tip down!

Aurora and Bunky added the soap powder, shut the door and turned the dial to START!

Working as a team was easy and fun, Bunky thought! He knew he had earned his dime this week, thanks to Aurora's help.
She was so nice.

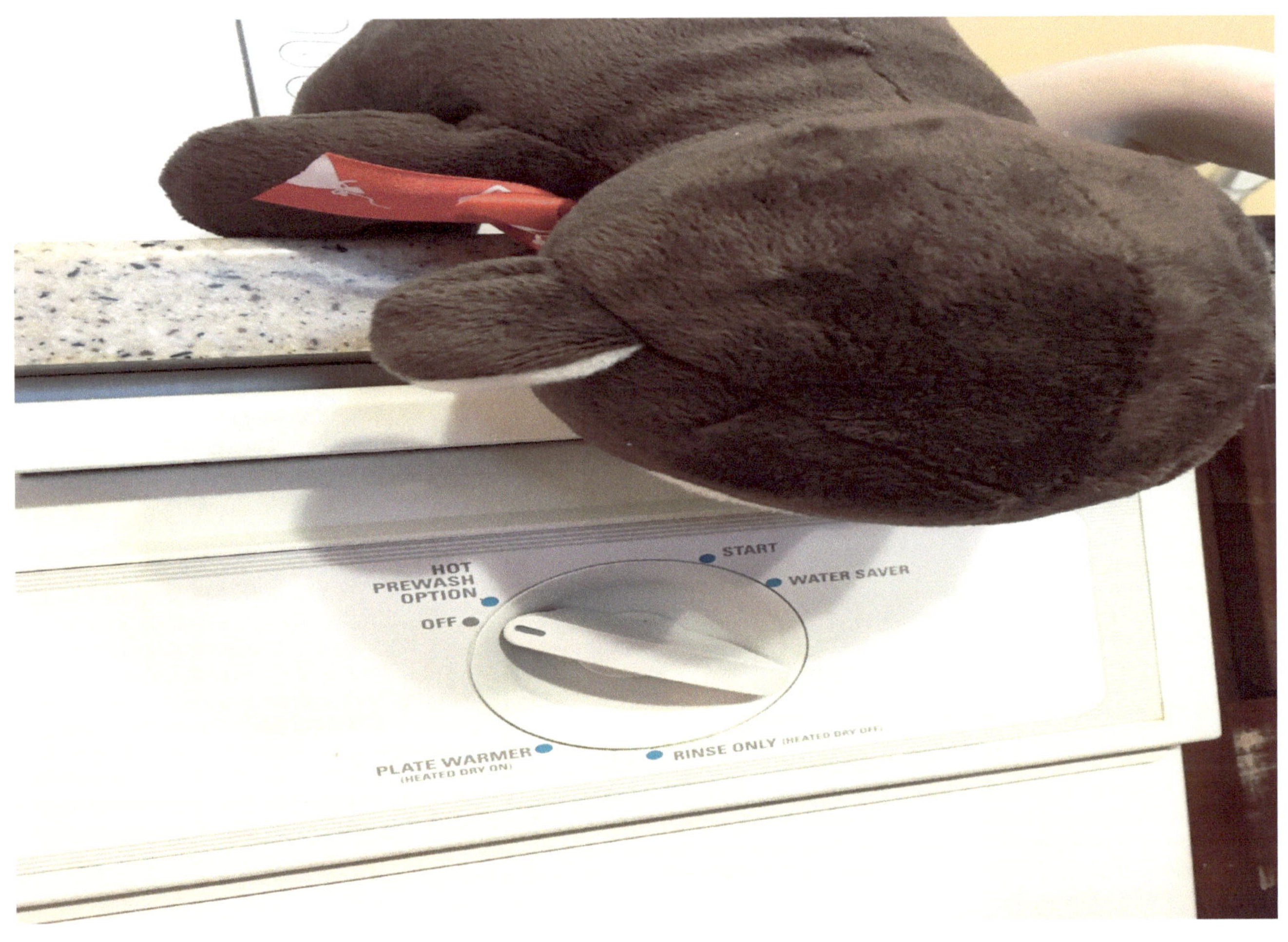

Bunky was also relieved he didn't have to do the (toilet) again! Yucky! Stinky!

Bunky was grateful for Jerry's willingness to switch chores and Aurora's cooperation. He could taste the ice cream already.

In 2 days, he'd be licking on his fresh, peach ice cream cone!!! Yum!

The End

(of another fruitful day!)

Keep an eye out for these other exciting Children's Books:

Penny the Enormous Python

Floyd the Colorful Chameleon

Francesca the Tropical Red-eyed Green Frog

Joe's Got Spots

Merrill the Squirrel and Jen the Hen:

Part 6 Brittany's Back!!!

Sydney (Cat)

Alice the Guinea Pig

Frances, a Gifted Frog for Sure!

Saffire. (Butterfly)

Serendipity. (Fish)

Jeremiah, the Song Bird

Christmas at the Castle

We are proud to introduce:

Frances,

a Gifted Frog for Sure!

Frances is a dreamer.

He is a green frog and he wants a draft horse of his own!!!

His, brother, Hal, said, "NO!"

Do you think Frances gave up his dream? Would you?

Read on and find out what really happened.

Also, introducing, Kathleen Fox, the magnificent artist!

Kathy made Frances come alive!

About the TrapStone LLC: Owner and Author…

My name is Miss Diane. I taught for 42 years and have read thousands of books aloud to children.

I enjoyed that so much, I decided to write and illustrate books for you myself.

Enjoy!!!

About the TrapStone LLC: Manager…
Ken Stone Sr. is a computer programmer and a business partner extraordinaire. He put my words, pictures and computer magic together so you could meet, Bunky Tries to do the Dishes.